Word Wise

Vol. One

Alison Brown

THE BANNER OF TRUTH TRUST

THE BANNER OF TRUTH TRUST
3 Murrayfield Road, Edinburgh EH12 6EL, UK
P.O. Box 621, Carlisle, PA 17013, USA

*

© Alison Brown 2009
First published 2009
Reprinted 2013

*

ISBN: 978 1 84871 027 6

*

Typeset in Arial 16/18 & 18/20 at
The Banner of Truth Trust,
Edinburgh

Printed in the USA by
Versa Press Inc.,
East Peoria, IL

*

With special thanks to
Aaron, Andrew, Cherith, Daniel,
Debbie, Leah, and Rachel (aged 8-11)
for their invaluable help.

Message from Heaven

Many years ago God sent a message to all the people who live on earth. It's a very important message which he wants the whole world to read! He didn't send it all at once. Instead he used over forty people who lived in different periods of time to write separate parts of it. Hundreds of years later all the parts were put together to make one great big book.

Today we call it the Bible (or Holy Scripture) and it is the most important book you will ever read! In 2 Timothy 3:16 we are told that every word of it came from God himself.

Find this verse in your Bible and write the first part of it here . . .

2 Tim. 3:16a

Why is the Bible different from all other writings?

....
....

The Bible is God's message to the world but it is also God's account of the world's history. That's why it's an amazing book!

Bible Writers

Nearly all of the Bible writers were Jewish. While they were writing they lived in various places and did very different jobs. There was a **shepherd**, a **farmer**, an army **commander**, a king's **cup-bearer**, a **doctor**, a tax-collector, a **tentmaker**, and several **fishermen**, as well as some **prophets**, **kings**, and more!

Their writings all agree, even though sometimes they were written hundreds of years apart. That is because each man wrote only the words that God the Holy Spirit wanted him to write. In those days they didn't have smooth white pages like those in our books. They wrote on pieces of thick paper called papyrus, which was made from pressed plant fibres.

The words in bold are hidden in the wordsearch. Can you find them?

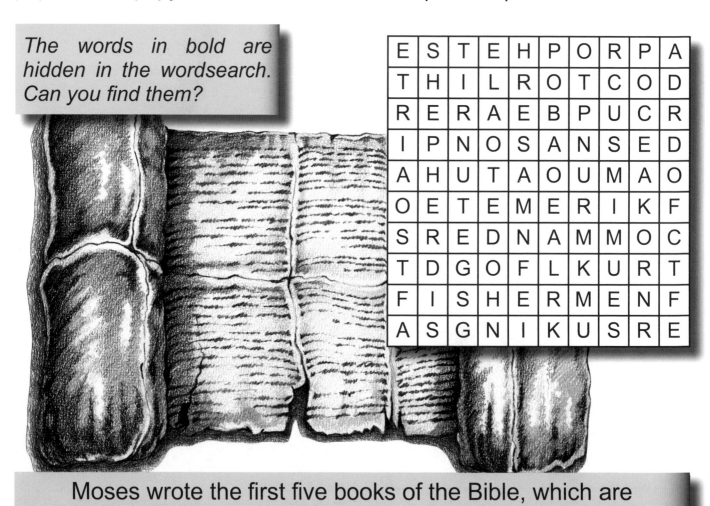

E	S	T	E	H	P	O	R	P	A
T	H	I	L	R	O	T	C	O	D
R	E	R	A	E	B	P	U	C	R
I	P	N	O	S	A	N	S	E	D
A	H	U	T	A	O	U	M	A	O
O	E	T	E	M	E	R	I	K	F
S	R	E	D	N	A	M	M	O	C
T	D	G	O	F	L	K	U	R	T
F	I	S	H	E	R	M	E	N	F
A	S	G	N	I	K	U	S	R	E

Moses wrote the first five books of the Bible, which are

....

....

Real Places

The Bible is full of true stories about real people and the things they did. Its towns, villages, rivers and mountains are all real places (although some names have changed since Bible times.)

If 1=A, 2=B, 3=C etc . . . find the names of ten Bible places we can still visit today!

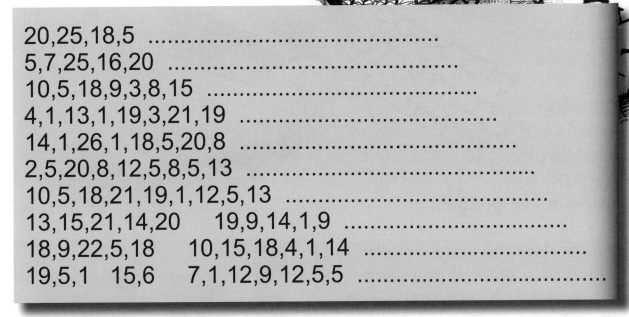

20,25,18,5 ....

5,7,25,16,20 ....

10,5,18,9,3,8,15 ....

4,1,13,1,19,3,21,19 ....

14,1,26,1,18,5,20,8 ....

2,5,20,8,12,5,8,5,13 ....

10,5,18,21,19,1,12,5,13 ....

13,15,21,14,20   19,9,14,1,9 ....

18,9,22,5,18   10,15,18,4,1,14 ....

19,5,1   15,6   7,1,12,9,12,5,5 ....

Archaeologists are people who dig up the sites of ancient towns and cities. Everything that archaeologists have discovered about life-styles, customs, kings, and battles agrees with what the Bible records. Nothing has ever been found which disagrees!

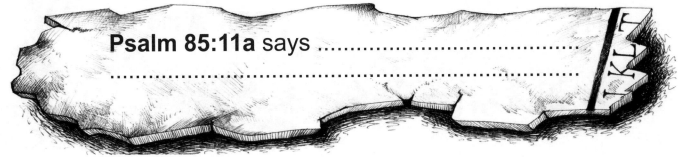

Psalm 85:11a says ....

....

Careful Copies

God has taken **great** care to **preserve** his own Word. Because the books of the Bible were first written on long strips of papyrus (or sometimes animal skins), they had to be rolled up. They were called **scrolls**, and when they became old and frayed and brittle new copies had to be made.

The **scribes** who did this were determined not to make **any** mistakes. They carefully **counted** the words and letters in each book to make **sure** nothing was added or left out or wrongly written.

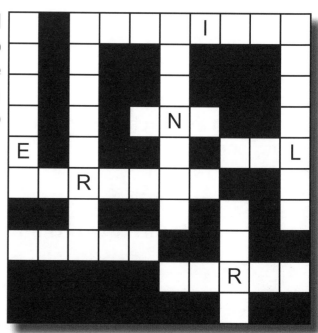

As the years passed hundreds of perfect copies were made. Later on printing was invented and thousands of **Bibles** were printed in many different languages.

The very important message which God wanted **all** the people of the world to read, was never lost or changed. Those early scribes knew that the **words** which God himself had spoken were much too **precious** to forget or lose.

Can you fit the words written in bold letters into the grid? Put the longest words in first.

Still the Same!

There was once a young shepherd .... who lived at a place called Qumran, on the shores of the Dead Sea, in the hot country of .... One day he was carelessly throwing stones into the mouth of a cave, when he heard the sound of pottery breaking. He crept inside to have a look and found some old dusty scrolls hidden in large clay .... They turned out to be very ancient copies of most of the .... of the Old Testament! The shepherd boy probably didn't understand just what a precious .... he had discovered!

Before that day the oldest copies of scripture dated from about 900 A.D. (That means 900 years after .... was born.) They were very old, but the scrolls found at the .... Sea, were much, much older! They had been written around 100 B.C. (about 1000 years earlier!).

Imagine how delighted Bible scholars were, when they found that the words in the older scrolls were almost exactly the .... as the words in their own newer scriptures.

Copies had been carefully made for a thousand .... without any serious mistakes!

WORD BANK

Jesus boy Dead
treasure same Israel
pots years books

Choose a word to fill each blank space above.

7

In the Beginning

The first book of the Bible describes how God created the earth.

> ### Write the words of **Genesis 1:1** here . . .
>
> ....
>
> ....

Scientists tell us that our world is made up of time, matter (material), and space. You will find a word to describe each of these in the very first verse of Genesis chapter 1.

Can you fill in the blanks?

Science	Genesis
Time	In the beginning
Space	the h ....
Matter	the e ....

Another very needful thing was energy and God provided that too when he spoke the simple words 'Let there be light.' God made everything in the proper order and nothing happened by accident. He designed all the plants and animals to produce more plants and animals just like themselves.

Check Genesis 1:1-27 What did God make on each day?

DAY ONE   Land, sea and plants
DAY TWO   Sun, moon and stars
DAY THREE   Animals and man
DAY FOUR   The atmosphere (firmament)
DAY FIVE   Light, day and night
DAY SIX   Sea creatures and birds

The First Family

In the book of Genesis we discover that people didn't come from animals or plants. God made man in his own image. That means that, unlike animals, each person has a soul that will live for ever.

We can read about the first husband and wife, Adam and Eve, who had a family of sons and daughters (Genesis 5:4). Everyone who has ever lived on earth comes from this family!

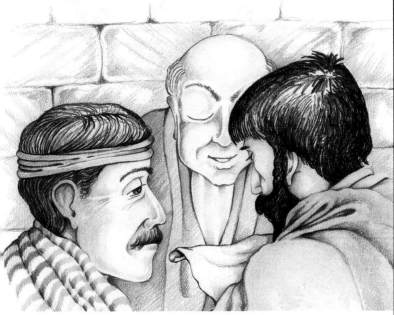

You can trace the descendants of Adam right down to Noah in Genesis chapter 5, and from Noah to Abraham in Genesis chapter 11 verses 10-32. Their life-spans, when all added together, account for the passing of thousands, not millions, of years.

Using Genesis 5 and Genesis 11 can you find the names which are missing from this list of Adam's descendants?

GEN.	
5:1	Adam
5:3	Seth
5:6	E ....
5:9	Cainan
5:12	M ....
5:15	Jared
5:18	E ....
5:21	Methuselah
5:25	L ....
5:29	Noah
5:32	S ....
GEN.	
11:10	Arphaxad
11:12	S ....
11:14	Eber
11:16	P ....
11:18	Reu
11:20	S ....
11:22	Nahor
11:24	T ....
11:26	Abraham

Spoiled by Sin

Genesis chapters 2 and 3 explain that at the **beginning** the world was simply **perfect**. The first two people, Adam and Eve, were close **friends** with God. God talked with them often and they loved his company too. God had said they must not eat the **fruit** of the tree called 'The Tree of the Knowledge of Good and Evil'. But they **disobeyed** him and ate the **forbidden** fruit.

A	B	D	A	F	E	O	L	A	N
T	E	E	L	R	N	S	U	P	E
C	P	Y	G	U	V	I	N	U	K
E	U	E	T	I	S	S	A	T	O
F	N	B	N	T	N	E	L	P	R
R	I	O	A	O	U	N	K	E	B
E	S	S	S	D	N	E	I	R	F
P	H	I	T	A	I	G	U	N	A
N	E	D	D	I	B	R	O	F	G
A	D	E	U	S	E	I	S	L	O

Because of that sin, the closeness between all mankind and God was **broken** (because God is utterly pure and holy). Sorrow and **pain** would enter into God's beautiful world. People would have to die as the result of sin and God said they would be **punished** even after death, through all eternity. Life on earth would not be like what God intended it to be.

The words in bold letters are hidden in the wordsearch.
Can you find them?

Romans 5:12 explains what happened. Write it here . . .

....

....

....

The Answer

God must have explained to this first family that the only way their sin could be forgiven was by shedding the blood of an animal. God had said the punishment for sin was death, but he would accept the death of a lamb instead of the death of a person. When they thought about this, those early people understood that sin was a very serious matter.

Romans 6:23a says ....
....
....

In Genesis we learn about two brothers who brought an offering to God. They knew that God had said they must offer an animal but the older brother, Cain, was careless.

Read Genesis 4:1-12, then unscramble the words below to make true sentences.

1. Cain his was a shepherd brother Abel farmer a was and
....

2. Cain an offering of fruit brought vegetables to God and
....

3. Abel the one of flock best lambs in God brought his to
....

4. Abel that lamb had to sin knew die a because of his
....

5. Cain to another find way to for tried pay his sin
....

6. God pleased with was but Cain displeased Abel with
....

7. Cain jealous brother later and killed was his Abel
....

World under Water

In Genesis chapter 6 we read that God was grieved as the (16,5,15,16,12,5) .... became more and more sinful. God had given them everything but they lived only to please themselves. They did very evil things all the time and God had to (16,21,14,9,19,8) .... them. There was only one man who loved God, and his name was Noah.

Genesis 6:9 says . . .

....
....
....
....

God gave Noah (5,24,1,3,20) .... instructions for building a (8,21,7,5) .... boat. God told him to warn the people that he was going to send a (20,5,18,18,9,2,12,5) .... flood because of their wickedness. Noah and his sons worked for a long time building the (23,15,15,4,5,14) .... ark.

Then they filled it with enough food to keep themselves and lots of (1,14,9,13,1,12,19) .... alive for a long time. They (16,12,5,1,4,5,4) .... with the people around them to come into the ark too but no-one would (12,9,19,20,5,14) .... When the ark was ready Noah and his family were the only people who would go inside. God sent a flood which completely (4,5,19,20,18,15,25,5,4) .... the earth and only the people who had believed God survived! God was gracious to them and kept them completely safe.

Bricks at Babel

A few hundred years after the flood the descendants of Noah became proud and sinful too. God had told them to spread out and fill up the beautiful earth he had made but they planned to do just the opposite and to worship other things instead of God!

First read the story in Genesis 11:1-9.

In those days everyone on the earth spoke the **same** language. The descendants of **Noah** found a flat plain in the land of **Shinar**. They made **bricks** and planned to build a huge **city** and a magnificent **tower** so that their name would always be remembered. They wouldn't obey or honour God.

So God **changed** their speech so that they could no longer understand or talk to each **other**. They had to separate and move away to new areas, just as God had intended at the beginning. The unfinished tower was later called **Babel**. The different **languages** in the world today all come from those early groups of people.

Can you fit the words in bold letters into the grid?

13

A New Nation

After the people began to settle in other parts of the world there was one man called Abraham who loved and honoured God. God called him aside and told him that he would be the beginning of a new nation (which was later called Israel). Abraham lived around 2000 years B.C. God said he was going to bless all the families of the world through him!

Look up the verses to complete the sentences.

Gen 12:1   God told Abraham to leave his ....

Gen 12:1   God would show him a .... to go to.

Gen 12:2   God would make him a great ....

Gen 12:3   In him all the .... of the earth would be blessed.

Gen 15:5   Abraham's descendants would be as countless as the .... in the sky.

Gen 17:19 His wife Sarah would have a son called ....

Gen 21:5   Isaac was born when Abraham was ....

Gen 24:67 Isaac married a girl called ....

Gen 25:27 Isaac's sons were called .... and Jacob.

Gen 29:18 Jacob wanted to marry a girl called ....

Gen 29:25 Jacob was tricked and had to marry .... too.

Gen 35:10 God changed Jacob's name to ....

Gen 35:22 Jacob had a total of .... sons.

Gen 37:3   Joseph, his favourite son, wore a special ....

Gen 41:41 Joseph became a ruler in the land of ....

Gen 46:6-7 Jacob and all his .... moved to Egypt.

Escape from Egypt

bless basket man difficult things throne Moses lead

For about 400 years the Israelites (the sons of Jacob and their children) lived in Egypt. Then a new Pharaoh came to the .... and he didn't like them! He thought there were far too many Israelites so he made them serve as slaves. They had to work long hours, toiling in the heat of the sun. How they longed to escape from this .... life!

One day the Pharaoh's daughter found an Israelite baby hidden in a .... among the reeds in the river Nile. She took him home to the palace and called him .... He was taught all the important .... that a prince should be taught.

Many years later, when baby Moses was a grown up .... , God called him to .... the Israelites out of the land of Egypt.

God helped them escape and also did many amazing miracles to prove, again and again, that he had not forgotten his promise to Abraham.

God was going to .... all the families on earth through these people, just as he had said he would!

Exodus (the second book of the Bible) describes how God brought the Israelites safely out of Egypt. **Leviticus** (the third book) then gives careful details of the laws God gave to his people.

Man is Sinful

On the way to the promised land (about 1400 B.C.) God met with Moses on Mount Sinai and gave him the Ten Commandments (See Exodus 20:1-17). When the Israelites thought about God's laws they began to understand just how sinful everyone really is!

What do the Ten Commandments teach us?

ACROSS

3. We are not to take the .... of the Lord our God in vain.

4. We are to keep the Sabbath .... holy.

5. We should honour our ....

7. We are not to commit ....

9. We are not to tell ....

10. We are not to .... what other people have.

DOWN

1. We are not to have any other .... before the Lord.

2. We are not to .... or worship an idol.

6. We are not to kill or commit ....

8. We are not to steal or .... things that don't belong to us.

God is Holy

The Israelites had many miles to go through hot desert to reach the (ndal) .... God had promised to them (called Canaan). They trusted God to provide them with food and (etrwa) .... and also to lead them in the (gtirh) .... direction.

God gave Moses instructions on how to make a beautiful (ntet) .... which they could carry with them. It was called the tabernacle. The pillars were covered with (ldog)................. and it had two (mroso) .... which were separated by a heavy, embroidered (evli) .... God's presence would dwell in the inner room which was called the Holy of Holies.

God said that the only way the (sni) .... of the people could be covered was by the shedding of (dolob) .... Only the High Priest was allowed to go through the veil into God's presence and he had to bring the blood of a (malb) .... God was reminding the Israelites that he cannot ignore sin. The punishment for sin is (dteha) .... When they thought about the animal that had (dedi) .... they knew that it had died in their (caple) .... and they were very thankful!

The book of **Numbers** describes the journey to Canaan.
Deuteronomy is a second telling of the laws of God.

Leaders of Israel

The next twelve books in the Bible are often called the history books! The Israelites finally entered the promised land (Canaan) just after Moses died. God chose Joshua next (see the book of **Joshua**), and then people like Deborah, Gideon and Samson, (in the book of **Judges**) to lead Israel against the Canaanites.

The book of **Ruth** tells the beautiful story of God's care for a girl who left the worship of idols to follow the God of Israel.

Then God's people were ruled by the great prophet Samuel (1 & 2 **Samuel**), and afterwards by various kings. Some of them loved God and some of them didn't! (See 1 & 2 **Kings** and 1 & 2 **Chronicles**.)

C	T	O	R	U	A	R	E	T	U
K	H	A	U	L	E	U	M	A	S
A	O	R	U	R	O	T	E	H	I
R	G	E	O	H	G	H	N	A	G
U	S	H	R	N	S	G	N	I	K
L	E	T	A	U	I	O	L	M	U
O	G	S	B	L	A	C	J	E	F
A	D	E	T	U	R	E	L	H	A
L	U	S	O	L	Z	A	I	E	D
E	J	G	A	F	E	T	O	N	S

Israel then disobeyed God. They were taken captive and their city, Jerusalem, was ruined but when we read the books of **Ezra** and **Nehemiah** we discover that later they got it back again and managed to rebuild the walls.

The last history book (**Esther**), tells of a queen who risked her own life to save God's people; it's an amazing story!

The book names are hidden in the wordsearch. Can you find them?

Words of Wisdom

At this point in the Bible we discover the books of wisdom (sometimes called the books of poetry). They contain songs, advice, thoughts and prayers written by different people. They cover all kinds of subjects such as creation, history, promises of things to come, and many of the writers' own personal experiences.

The first book is thought to be the oldest in the Bible and dates from before the writings of Moses. The next four were written mainly by two of the Kings of Israel—David and Solomon.

If (1,1)=A, (2,1)=B, (3,1)=C etc… can you work out the names of the books of wisdom?

5	U	V	W	X	Y
4	P	Q	R	S	T
3	K	L	M	N	O
2	F	G	H	I	J
1	A	B	C	D	E
	1	2	3	4	5

(5,2)(5,3)(2,1)

....

(1,4)(4,4)(1,1)(2,3)(3,3)(4,4)

....

(1,4)(3,4)(5,3)(2,5)(5,1)(3,4)(2,1)(4,4)

....

(5,1)(3,1)(3,1)(2,3)(5,1)(4,4)(4,2)(1,1)(4,4)(5,4)(5,1)(4,4)

....

(4,4)(5,3)(4,3)(2,2) (5,3)(1,2) (4,4)(5,3)(2,3)(5,3)(3,3)(5,3)(4,3)

....

Warnings from God

The final books of the Old Testament were written by prophets. The prophets lived mainly in the days of the kings (about 1000 B.C. to 400 B.C.) and were men chosen by God to give his messages to the people of Israel. They warned that God would not let sin go unpunished!

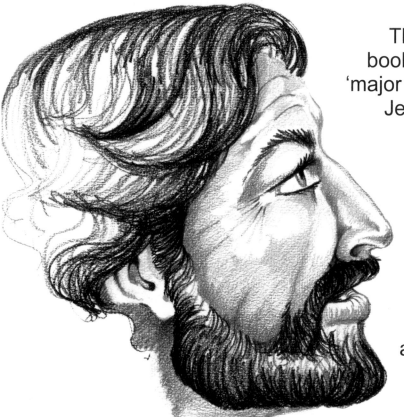

Those who wrote the first five books are sometimes called the 'major prophets'. They are Isaiah, Jeremiah, Ezekiel and Daniel.

Jeremiah wrote two books. His second one was called 'Lamentations' because he was lamenting or mourning the sinful state of Israel.

Sometimes God gave the prophets visions or dreams about things that would take place many centuries later!

Can you unscramble these words to make true sentences?

1. The Testament books of last the Old wrote prophets the

....

2. The lived the prophets around time the kings as same

....

3. Prophets God's gave to messages people the Israel of

....

4. The Jeremiah the wrote prophet of Lamentations book

....

5. Sometimes the gave visions God about the prophets future

....

The King is Coming!

The prophets who wrote the twelve shorter books at the very end of the Old Testament are known as the 'minor prophets'.

Look in the index of your Bible and find the prophets' names missing from this list.

Hosea
J ....
Amos
O ....
J ....
Micah
N ....
H ....
Z ....
H ....
Zechariah
M ....

God gave the prophets details about the blessing that would come to the whole world through Israel. God would send a very special person down to earth. He would be the greatest Prophet, Priest, and King the world has ever known. He would show men how to prepare for the future, he would pay the price for their sin, and one day he would rule the world in righteousness! What a blessing!

What did God tell the prophet Zechariah about the wonderful Person who would come?

Zechariah 9:9 says ....
....
....
....

Old Testament Review

BOOKS OF MOSES
G............................
E............................
Leviticus
N............................
D............................

HISTORY BOOKS
J............................
J............................
R............................
1&2 S........................
1&2 K........................
1&2 Chronicles
E............................
N............................
E............................

BOOKS OF WISDOM
J............................
P............................
P............................
Ecclesiastes
S............................

MAJOR PROPHETS
I............................
J............................
Lamentations
E............................
D............................

MINOR PROPHETS
H............................
J............................
A............................
O............................
J............................
M............................
N............................
H............................
Zephaniah
H............................
Z............................
M............................

Do you know all the books of the Old Testament?

With the help of the previous pages can you complete this list?

Good News!

After the prophets fell silent Israel was invaded by the Romans. In 63 B.C. Herod was made king of Judea, and then … God kept his **promise**! God **himself** came down to earth (in the person of his Son, the Lord Jesus Christ). Jesus was to be the sacrifice for sin that all people need. Some people who knew **Jesus** were inspired by the Holy Spirit to write about him, so that **all** the world could hear about God's wonderful **gift**.

They wrote about his **birth** in the little town of Bethlehem, his **ministry** all over Israel, and then his **death**, outside the city of Jerusalem.

The writers of the first four books of the New Testament were men called Matthew, Mark, Luke, and John. Their books are known as the Gospels which means 'good news'. The message contained in them is simply the most wonderful **news** that the world has ever been told! God has sent an **answer** for the big problem of sin.

Can you fit the words in bold letters into the grid?

News for the Jews

If 1=A, 2=B, 3=C etc. can you fill in the missing words?

The people of Israel became known as the Jews. They had been waiting for many years for God to send the promised king. Some Jews were very (5,24,3,9,20,5,4) .... when Jesus was born because they thought he would be like other kings and help them to (4,5,6,5,1,20) .... all their enemies.

Matthew wrote his book especially for the (10,5,23,19) .... He wanted to (16,18,15,22,5) .... to them that Jesus really was their King. The first question we meet in his book is, 'Where is he who is born King of the Jews?'

Kings must have royal blood so Matthew explains that Jesus was descended from King (4,1,22,9,4) .... He was visited by (18,15,25,1,12,20,25) .... after his birth and they even brought him royal gifts.

Matthew's Gospel also describes how Jesus was dressed as a king before he died. He wore a purple (18,15,2,5) .... and a crown of (20,8,15,18,14,19) .... was placed on his head. The title, 'King of the Jews', was written above him for all to see.

The word 'kingdom' is used over (6,9,6,20,25) .... times in Matthew's book. Jesus Christ, the Son of God, would be the King of kings through all (5,20,5,18,14,9,20,25) ....!

News for the Romans

Israel was now under Roman rule so there were Roman soldiers and centurions in the towns and streets. Mark wrote his book so that they too would understand who Jesus was.

He didn't talk about Jesus' family tree … because he knew Romans wouldn't be interested in the background of a simple Jewish servant who came from a place called Nazareth.

Instead Mark wrote about the things that Jesus did, the miracles he performed and the many sick people who were healed. The Romans would be impressed to hear of a servant who gave his life for others … and even died for them!

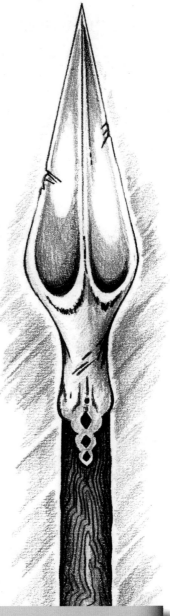

5	U	V	W	X	Y
4	P	Q	R	S	T
3	K	L	M	N	O
2	F	G	H	I	J
1	A	B	C	D	E
	1	2	3	4	5

If (1,1)=A, (2,1)=B, (3,1)=C etc… can you make some words used in the book of Mark, to describe the Lord Jesus?

(5,4)(3,2)(5,1)   (3,1)(1,1)(3,4)(1,4)(5,1)(4,3)(5,4)(5,1)(3,4)

....

(5,4)(3,2)(5,1)   (4,4)(5,3)(4,3)   (5,3)(1,2)   (3,3)(1,1)(3,4)(5,5)

....

(1,1)   (1,4)(3,4)(5,3)(1,4)(3,2)(5,1)(5,4)

....

(5,4)(3,2)(5,1)   (3,1)(3,2)(3,4)(4,2)(4,4)(5,4)

....

News for the Greeks

Luke, the writer of the third Gospel book, wasn't a Jew himself, so he was writing for non-Jews (mainly Greeks). Luke was a (todcor) .... and he cared about (eelopp) .... He cared especially about the lonely widows, the sick, the hungry, the unloved and the (eendy) .... all around him.

When Luke was writing about the (tribh) .... of Jesus he described the humble stable in Bethlehem and the visit, not of the kings, but of ordinary (hesprhsde) ....

Luke wanted everyone to know that Jesus didn't just come to help the wealthy. Jesus understood what it was like to be (roop) ....

Luke was the (yoln) .... Gospel writer to tell the stories of The Prodigal Son and Zacchaeus. He knew that sinful people feel (ahmdsae) .... and despised and he wanted them to know that Jesus still loved those who had stolen (emoyn) .... or acted shamefully. Both these stories show how willing Jesus was to (frgovei) .... sinful men. Luke painted a picture of a Redeemer, who came to save not just the Jews, but (anoyne) .... who would call upon him!

Luke 19:10 says ....
....

News for the World

John was one of the twelve disciples of Jesus. He had left the .... business to follow Christ and he was called the disciple 'whom Jesus loved'. He wrote his .... because he wanted the whole .... to know that Jesus was not just a king, a .... and a healer, but the Son of God.

John 20:31 says ....

....

....

John is the only Gospel writer to record what Jesus said just before he .... on the cross. The words 'It is finished' are very precious to us today because they mean that, at that moment, the price for sin was completely paid! .... was the Lamb who .... his blood and gave his life. God gave his only Son so that we may be forgiven and .... the punishment that we really deserve.

John 3:16 says ....

....

....

....

The Early Church

Luke also wrote the book called the Acts of the Apostles. After Jesus had risen from the dead he met with all his disciples before he returned to heaven. God then sent the Holy Spirit down to earth to help the believers. The Holy Spirit gave the disciples the ability to preach, even in languages they hadn't known before!

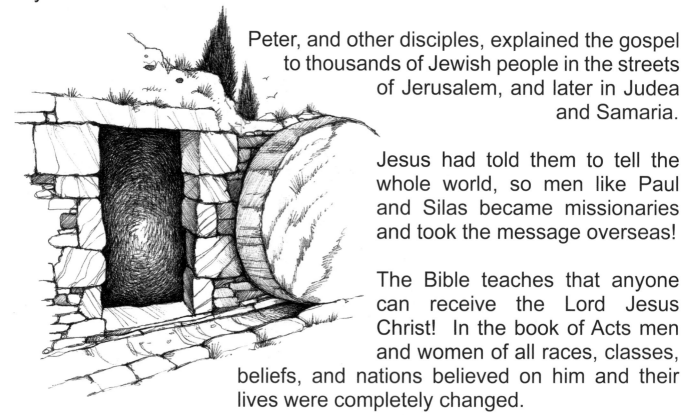

Peter, and other disciples, explained the gospel to thousands of Jewish people in the streets of Jerusalem, and later in Judea and Samaria.

Jesus had told them to tell the whole world, so men like Paul and Silas became missionaries and took the message overseas!

The Bible teaches that anyone can receive the Lord Jesus Christ! In the book of Acts men and women of all races, classes, beliefs, and nations believed on him and their lives were completely changed.

Unscramble the words below to make true sentences.

1. The of written was Luke book by a doctor Acts called

....

2. It did what Jesus he describes after arose the dead from

....

3. Disciples by the led were Holy to preach Spirit gospel the

....

4. Missionaries to sent preach in were countries other

....

5. People any receive or language of can nation Jesus

....

The Letters

The next Bible books are made up of letters written by some of the early believers. Groups of Christians had joined together to form little churches, and the apostles wrote to encourage many of them. Paul wrote to the **Romans**, **Corinthians**, **Galatians**, **Ephesians**, **Philippians**, **Colossians**, and **Thessalonians**. We also find letters from Paul to his friends **Timothy**, **Titus,** and **Philemon. Hebrews** was written to Jewish Christians who were suffering for their faith in the Lord Jesus Christ. Finally there are letters written by **James**, **Peter**, **John,** and **Jude** to other believers. The letters are filled with helpful teaching about what it means to be a Christian.

Can you find the names of all the letter books in the wordsearch?

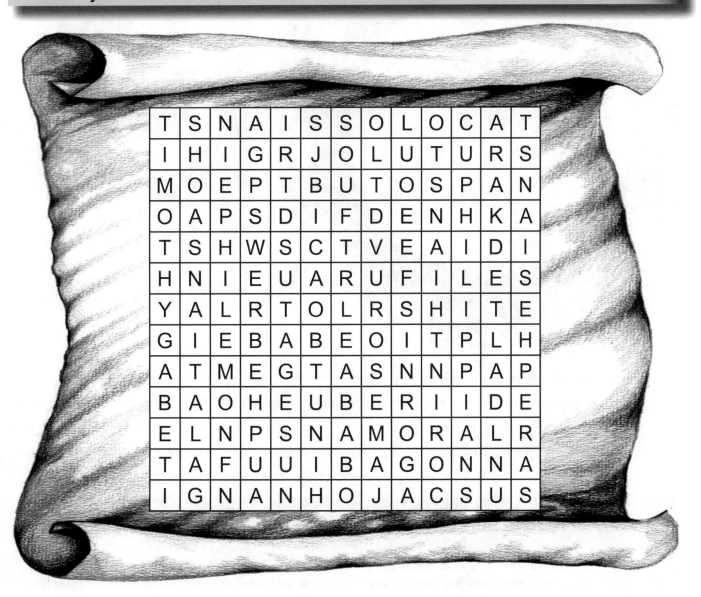

T	S	N	A	I	S	S	O	L	O	C	A	T
I	H	I	G	R	J	O	L	U	T	U	R	S
M	O	E	P	T	B	U	T	O	S	P	A	N
O	A	P	S	D	I	F	D	E	N	H	K	A
T	S	H	W	S	C	T	V	E	A	I	D	I
H	N	I	E	U	A	R	U	F	I	L	E	S
Y	A	L	R	T	O	L	R	S	H	I	T	E
G	I	E	B	A	B	E	O	I	T	P	L	H
A	T	M	E	G	T	A	S	N	N	P	A	P
B	A	O	H	E	U	B	E	R	I	I	D	E
E	L	N	P	S	N	A	M	O	R	A	L	R
T	A	F	U	U	I	B	A	G	O	N	N	A
I	G	N	A	N	H	O	J	A	C	S	U	S

The King will Return!

The last book of the Bible, the **Revelation**, was written by John in his old age. It is a book of **hope** and encouragement to believers. Although the world is a very evil place to live in, yet at God's appointed time the Lord Jesus **Christ** will suddenly appear again on the earth. Those who have loved and obeyed him will **rejoice**! They will **praise** him with joyful songs of thankfulness. He is the King of kings and **Lord** of lords and no-one who fights against him will succeed. Jesus will reign victorious for **ever** and ever!

The book of Revelation brings a warning too. **Jesus** will also return as the judge over everyone who has ever lived on earth. Those who have loved Jesus as their **Saviour** and whose names are found written in the Book of **Life**, will not be punished, because Jesus took the punishment for their sins already. They will live with him in heaven (the New Jerusalem) for all eternity. But those who did not trust in Jesus to forgive their sins will be sent to a place of terrible punishment for ever and ever (Revelation 20:11-15).

Can you fit the words in bold letters into the grid?

New Testament Review

THE GOSPELS

M ....

M ....

Luke

J ....

CHURCH HISTORY

A ....

THE LETTERS

R ....

1&2 C ....

G ....

E ....

P ....

C ....

1&2 Thessalonians

1&2 T ....

T ....

P ....

H ....

J ....

1&2 P ....

1,2&3 John

J ....

PROPHECY

R ....

With the help of the previous pages can you fill in the blanks below?

John 21:25 says ....
....
....
....
....
....
....

31

God's Amazing Book is the outcome
of many years of creating and illustrating
puzzle pages for use in my Sunday School
Class and a church magazine. Designed with
the aim of teaching children biblical truth, I pray
that it will also encourage them to want to become wise
in God's Holy Word. Some children, less familiar with the Bible,
may need help to locate the Scripture references . . .
but time taken to do this will be time well spent.

. . . that they may learn to fear me all the days that they shall live upon the earth
and that they may teach their children
Deuteronomy 4:10